I0158369

THE DEDICATION

To those that do delight in Scenes and wit,
I dedicate my Book, for those I writ;
Next to my own Delight, for I did take
Much pleasure and delight these Playes to make;
For all the time my Playes a making were,
My brain the Stage, my thoughts were acting there.

TO THE LADY MARCHIONESS OF NEWCASTLE UPON HER PLAYES

Terence and Plautus Wits we now do scorn,
Their Comick Socks worn out, in pieces torn,
Only their rags of Wit remain as toyes
For Pedants to admire, to teach School Boyes;
It is not time hath wasted all their Fame,

But your high Phancies, and your nobler flame,
Which burnt theirs up in their own ashes lies,
Nor Phoenix like e'r out of those will rise;
Old Tragick Buskins now are thrown away,
When we read your each Passion in each Play,
No stupid block or stony heart forbears
To drown their Cheeks in Seas of salter Tears;
Such power you have in Tragick, Comick stile,
When for to fetch a tear or make a smile,
Still at your pleasure all our passions ly
Obedient to your pen, to laugh or cry;
So even with the thread of Natures fashion,
As you play on her heart-strings still of passion;
So we are all your Subjects in each Play,
Unwilling willingly still to obey;
Or have a thought but what you make or draw
Us by the power of your wits great law;
Thus Emperess in Soveraign power yours sits
Over the wise, and tames Poetick wits.

W. Newcastle.

CAST LIST

The Lord Fatherly
The Lord Singularity
His Sonne
Sir Serious Dumbe
Sir Timothy Complement
Sir Humphry Bolde
Sir Roger Exception
Sir Peaceable Studious
Foster Trusty
The Lady Orphant
The Lady Ignorant wife to Sir Peaceable Studious
The Lady Bashfull
The Lady Wagtaile
The Lady Amorous
Mrs. Acquaintance
Nurse Hondly Foster Trusties wife
Lady Orphans Nurse
Mrs. Reformers woman to the Lady Bashfull
Two Chamber-Maydes

PROLOGUE

Loves Adventures by Margaret Cavendish

Part I (of II)

Margaret Lucas Cavendish, Duchess of Newcastle-upon-Tyne was born in 1623 in Colchester, Essex into a family of comfortable means.

As the youngest of eight children she spent much time with her siblings. Margaret had no formal education but she did have access to scholarly libraries and tutors, although she later said the children paid little attention to the tutors, who were there 'rather for formality than benefit'.

From an early age Margaret was already assembling her thoughts for future works despite the then conditions of society that women did not partake in public authorship. For England it was also a time of Civil War. The Royalists were being pushed back and Parliamentary forces were in the ascendancy.

Despite these obvious dangers, when Queen Henrietta Maria was in Oxford, Margaret asked her mother for permission to become one of her Ladies-in-waiting. She was accepted and, in 1644, accompanied the Queen into exile in France. This took her away from her family for the first time.

Despite living at the Court of the young King Louis XIV, life for the young Margaret was not what she expected. She was far from her home and her confidence had been replaced by shyness and difficulties fitting in to the grandeur of her surroundings and the eminence of her company.

Margaret told her mother she wanted to leave the Court. Her mother was adamant that she should stay and not disgrace herself by leaving. She provided additional funds for her to make life easier. Margaret remained. It was now also that she met and married William Cavendish who, at the time, was the Marquis of Newcastle (and later Duke). He was also 30 years her senior and previously married with two children.

As Royalists, a return to life in England was not yet possible. They would remain in exile in Paris, Rotterdam and Antwerp until the restoration of the crown in 1660 although Margaret was able to return for attention to some estate matters.

Along with her husband's brother, Sir Charles Cavendish, she travelled to England after having been told that her husband's estate (taken from him due to his being a royalist) was to be sold and that she, as his wife, would receive some benefit of the sale. She received nothing. She left England to be with her husband again.

The couple were devoted to each other. Margaret wrote that he was the only man she was ever in love with, loving him not for title, wealth or power, but for merit, justice, gratitude, duty, and fidelity. She also relied upon him for support in her career. The marriage provided no children despite efforts made by her physician to overcome her inability to conceive.

Margaret's first book, 'Poems and Fancies', was published in 1653; it was a collection of poems, epistles and prose pieces which explores her philosophical, scientific and aesthetic ideas.

For a woman at this time writing and publishing were avenues they had great difficulty in pursuing. Added to this was Margaret's range of subjects. She wrote across a number of issues including gender, power, manners, scientific method, and philosophy.

She always claimed she had too much time on her hands and was therefore able to indulge her love of writing. As a playwright she produced many works although most are as closet dramas. (This is a play not intended to be performed onstage, but instead read by a solitary reader or perhaps out loud in a small group. For Margaret the rigours of exile, her gender and Cromwell's closing of the theatres mean this was her early vehicle of choice and, despite these handicaps, she became one of the most well-known playwrights in England)

Her utopian romance, 'The Blazing World', (1666) is one of the earliest examples of science fiction. Margaret also published extensively in natural philosophy and early modern science; at least a dozen books.

She was the first woman to attend a meeting at Royal Society of London in 1667 and she criticized and engaged with members and philosophers Thomas Hobbes, René Descartes, and Robert Boyle.

Margaret was always defended against any criticism by her husband and he also contributed to some of her works. She also gives him credit as her writing tutor.

Perhaps a little strangely she said her ambition despite her shyness, was to have everlasting fame. During her career, from the mid 1650's until her death, she was prolific. In recent decades her work has undergone a resurgence of interest propelled mainly by her ground-breaking attitude and accomplishments in those male straitened times.

Margaret Cavendish died on 15th December 1673 and was buried at Westminster Abbey.

Index of Contents

Noble Spectators, you are come to see,
A Play, if good, perchance may clapped be;
And yet our Authoresse sayes that she hath heard,
Some playes, though good, hath not been so preferr'd;
As to be mounted up on high raised praise,
And to be Crown'd with Garlands of fresh hayes:
But the contrary have been hissed off,
Out from our Stage with many a censuring scoff;
But afterwards there understanding cleer'd,
They gave the praise, what they before had jeer'd.
The same she sayes may to her Play befall,
And your erroneous censures may recall:
But all such Playes as take not at first sight,
But afterwards the viewers takes delight:
It seemes there is more wit in such a Play,
Than can be understood in one whole day:
If for, she is well content for her wits sake,
From ignorance repulses for to take;
For she had rather want those understanding braines,
Than that her Play should want wits flowing veynes.

ACT I

SCENE I

[Enter the **LORD FATHERLY**, and the **LORD SINGULARITY** his Son.

LORD SINGULARITY
Pray, Sir, do not force me to marry a childe, before you know whether she will prove vertuous, or discreet; when for the want of that knowledge, you may indanger the honour of your Line and Posterity, with Cuckoldry and Bastardry.

LORD FATHERLY
Son, you must leave that to fortune.

LORD SINGULARITY
A wise man, Sir, is to be the maker or spoiler of his own fortune.

LORD FATHERLY
Let me tell you Son, the wisest man that is, or ever was, may be deceived in the choosing a wife, for a woman is more obscure than nature her self, therefore you must trust to chance, for marriage is a Lottery, if you get a prize, you may live quietly and happily.

LORD SINGULARITY

But if I light of a blank, as a hundred to one, nay a thousand to one but I shall, which is on a Fool or a Whore, her Follies or Adulteries, instead of a praise, will sound out my disgrace.

LORD FATHERLY
Come, Come, she is Rich, she is Rich.

LORD SINGULARITY
Why Sir, guilded Horns are most visible.

LORD FATHERLY
'Tis better, Son, to have a rich whore than a poor whore, but I hope Heaven hath made her Chast, and her Father being an honourable, honest, and wise man, will breed her vertuously, and I make no question but you will be happy with her.

LORD SINGULARITY
But Sir, pray consider the inequality of our ages, she being but a Child, and I at mans Estate; by that time she is ready for the marriage bed: I shall be ready for the grave, and youths sharp appetites, will never rellish Age, wherefore she will seek to please her pallat else where.

LORD FATHERLY
Let me tell you, Son, should you marry a woman that were as many years older, than she is younger than you; it were a greater hazard, for first old women are more intemperate than young: and being older than the husband, they are apt to be jealouse, and being jealouse, they grow malitious, and malice seeks revenge, and revenge disgrace, therefore she would Cuckold you meerly to disgrace you.

LORD SINGULARITY
On the other side, those Women that are marryed young, Cuckholds there Husbands fames dishonouring them by their ignorant follyes, and Childish indiscretions, as much as with Adultery. And I should as soon choose to be a Cuckhold, as to be thought to be one: For my honour will suffer as much by the one as the other, if not more.

LORD FATHERLY
Heaven blesse the, Sonne, from jealousy, for thou art horrible afraid of being a Cuckold.

LORD SINGULARITY
Can you blame me, Sir, since to be a Cuckhold is to be despised, scorned, laught, and pointed at, as a Monster worse than nature ever made, and all the Honour that my birth gave me and my education indued me, my vertue gained me, my industry got me; fortune bestowed on me, and fame inthron'd me for: may not only be lost by my wifes Adultery, but as I said by her indiscretion; which makes me wonder, how any man that hath a Noble Soul, dares marry since all his honour lyes or lives in the light heels of his wife, which every little passion is apt to kick away, wherefore good Sir, let me live a single life.

LORD FATHERLY
How Son, would you have me consent to extinguish the light of my Name, and to pull out the root of my posterity.

LORD SINGULARITY

Why Sir, it were better to lye in dark oblivion, than to have a false light to devulge your disgrace; and you had better pull out the root, than to have a branch of dishonour ingrafted therein.

LORD FATHERLY
All these Arguments against Marriage is, because you would injoy your Mistresses with freedom; fearing you should be disturbed by a wife.

LORD SINGULARITY
That needs not; for I observe, married Men takes as much liberty, if not more than Batchellors; for Batchellors are affraid they should challenge a promise of Marriage, and married Men are out of that danger.

LORD FATHERLY
Then that is the reason that Batchellors Court Married wives, and Married Men Courts Maides; but howsoever Son, if all Men should be of your mind, there would be no Marring nor giving in Marriage; but all must be in Common.

LORD SINGULARITY
That were best Sir, for then there could be no Adultery committed, or Cuckolds made.

LORD FATHERLY
For shame take courage, and be not a fraid of a Woman.

LORD SINGULARITY
By Heaven Sir, I would sooner yield up my life to death, than venture my honour to a womans management.

LORD FATHERLY
Well Son, I shall not force you with threates or commands to marry against your will and good likeing; but I hope Heaven will turn your mind towards marriage, and send thee a loving, vertuous and discreet wife.

SCENE II

[Enter the **LADY WAGTAILE**, the **LADY AMOROUS**, **SIR TIMOTHY COMPLEMENT**, **SIR HUMPHREY BOLD**, and **SIR ROGER EXCEPTION**.

SIR TIMOTHY COMPLEMENT
Bright beauty, may I be your Servant.

LADY AMOROUS
If I have any beauty, it was begot in your Eyes. And takes light from your commendations.

SIR TIMOTHY COMPLEMENT
You are Lady, the Starre of your Sex.

LADY AMOROUS

No truely, I am but a Meteor that soon goeth out.

LADY WAGTAILE
Preethy Sir Timothy Compliment, and Lady Amorous, do not stand prating here, but let us go a broad to some place to devert the time.

LADY AMOROUS
Dear Wagtaile, whether shall we goe?

SIR TIMOTHY COMPLEMENT
Faith let us go to a Play.

SIR HUMPHREY BOLD
Let's go to a Tavern.

SIR ROGER EXCEPTION
What with Ladyes!

SIR HUMPHREY BOLD
Why, Ladyes have been in Tavernes before now.

SIR ROGER EXCEPTION
It were as good to carry them to a Bawdy-house.

SIR HUMPHREY BOLD
As good say you, faith now I think of it, better; it were the only place to pass a way idle time. Come Ladyes shall we go.

LADY AMOROUS
Whether?

SIR HUMPHREY BOLD
To a Bawdy-house.

LADY AMOROUS
O fye! fye! Sir Humphrey Bold ; how wantonly you talk?

LADY WAGTAILE
But would you carry us in good earnest to a Bawdy-house?

SIR HUMPHREY BOLD
Why, do you question it, when every house is a secret Bawdy-house. Na! Let me tell you, there be many Right Worshipfull, Nay, Right Honourable, and most Noble Pallaces made Bawdy-houses.

SIR ROGER EXCEPTION
Some perchance that are old and ruinous, and the right owners out.

SIR HUMPHREY BOLD

No, some that are new, large, and finely furnished; and the owners stately, proud, scornfull, and jeering, living therein.

SIR ROGER EXCEPTION
They should take heed of jeering, least they be jeered; and of being scornfull, least they be scorned.

SIR HUMPHREY BOLD
What say you Ladyes, are you resolved.

LADY WAGTAILE
No, No, we will not go with you to such places now; but I will carry you to a young Lady whose Father is newly dead, and hath left her all his Estate; and she is become a great heir.

SIR ROGER EXCEPTION
Perchance Lady she will not receive our visit, if her Father be newly dead.

LADY WAGTAILE
I perceive you are ignorant of Funerall customes, for widdowes, heires, and heiresses receives visits whilst the Corpes lyes above ground: And they will keep them so much the longer, to have so many more visitants: nay, sometimes they will keep them so long, as there dissembling is perceived, or so long as they stink above ground; for if they bury not the Corpes and set empty Coffins for want of imbalming, their miserableness will stench up the Nostrils of their vanity.

SIR ROGER EXCEPTION
Nay by your favour Lady, there are some that are buried whilst they are steeming hot.

SIR HUMPHREY BOLD
Those are only such whose Executors, widdowes, or widdowers, feares they may revive again, and rather than that they should do so, they will bury them alive.

LADY WAGTAILE
You say rightly true, Sir Humphrey Bold.

SIR TIMOTHY COMPLEMENT
Sweet beautyes, let us go to see this Rich heiress.

LADY AMOROUS
Content.

SIR ROGER EXCEPTION
But Ladyes are you acquainted with her.

LADY WAGTAILE
O no! But you may know that all women rather than want visits, they will go to those they never saw, nor spoak to: but only heares of them; and where they live, and I can direct the Coachman to this Ladyes Lodging, wherefore let us go.

SIR HUMPHREY BOLD

I shall not deny to visit a Rich heiress.

SIR ROGER EXCEPTION
I shall waite upon you Ladyes, but—

LADY WAGTAILE
Nay, never make buts, but let's go.

LADY AMOROUS
Pray let us call Sir Serious Dumb, to go along with us.

LADY WAGTAILE
Faith Amorous you love his Company, because he can tell no tales.

SIR HUMPHREY BOLD
Pray call him not, but let him alone: for I dare sweare he is inventing of some useless and foolish Art.

SIR TIMOTHY COMPLEMENT
Is he so inventive say you, but if his inventions is useless, he invents in vain.

SIR ROGER EXCEPTION
Why may not a Dumb mans Inventions be as good as a blind, for the most usefullest Artes were invented, as the learned saith, by one born blind.

LADY WAGTAILE
Me thinks a dumb man should not have much wit, for by my troath one that is dumb seemes to me like a fool; nay, one that speakes but little: I cannot for my life but condemn him, or her for an Ass.

SIR HUMPHREY BOLD
He may be a fool, although he may chance to light on some inventions; for Artes are oftner produced from chance than wit, but let us go and leave him.

LADY WAGTAILE [Whispers to **SIR HUMPHREY BOLD**]
Faith Sir Humphrey Bold, we must call him, or otherwise my friend Amorous will be out of humour.

SIR HUMPHREY BOLD
Doth she love silence so well.

LADY WAGTAILE
No, no, it is that she loves secrecy so well.

[Exit.

CHORUS
In a minutes time is flown
From a Child, to Woman grown;
Some will smile, or laughing say;
This is but a foolish Play;

By Reason a Comedy, should of one dayes action be,
Let them laugh and so will I
At there great simplicity;
I as other Poets brings
Severall Nations, Subjects, Kings
All to Act upon one stage,
So severall times in one Age.

SCENE III

[Enter the **LADY ORPHANT**, and **MRS ACQUAINTANCE**.

MRS ACQUAINTANCE
How do you know the Lord Singularity is such a gallant man? For he hath been out of the Kingdom this 7 yeares; wherefore, you could have no acquaintance, you being yet very young.

LADY ORPHANT
Although I have no acquaintance by sight, or experienced knowledge; yet by report I have: for I remembred I heard my Father say, he was the honour of the Age, the glory of our Nation; and a pattern for all mankind to take a sample from, and that his person was answerable to his merrits, for he said he was a very handsome man, of a Masculine presence, a Courtly garbe, and affable and courteous behaviour; and that his wit was answerable to his merits, person, and behaviour, as that he had a quick wit, a solid judgment, a ready tongue and a smooth speech.

MRS ACQUAINTANCE
And did your Father proffer you to be his wife.

LADY ORPHANT
Yes, and I remember my father sighing said, he should have died in peace, and his soul would have rested in quiet, if he had been pleased to have accepted of me.

MRS ACQUAINTANCE
When did your Father proffer you.

LADY ORPHANT
When I was but a Child.

MRS ACQUAINTANCE
He is not married, and therefore he may chance to accept of you now, if you were profer'd.

LADY ORPHANT
That were but to be refused again, for I heare he is resolved never to marry, and it will be a greater disgrace to be refused now I am grown to womans Estate, than when I was but a Child, besides my Father is dead, and my marring can give him no content in the grave; unless his soul could view the world and the severall actions therein.

MRS ACQUAINTANCE
So, is his Father dead.

LADY ORPHANT
Yes, and I here that is the cause he cares not to return into his native Country.

MRS ACQUAINTANCE
I have a friend that hath his picture.

LADY ORPHANT
Is it a he or a she friend.

MRS ACQUAINTANCE
A she friend.

LADY ORPHANT
Pray be so much my friend, as to get your friends consent to shew me the Picture.

MRS ACQUAINTANCE
Perchance I may get it to view it my self, but I shall never perswade her to lend it you, jealousy will forbid her.

LADY ORPHANT
She hath no cause to fear me, for I am not one to make an Amorous Mrs. and I have heard he will never marry.

MRS ACQUAINTANCE
That is all one; woman hath hopes as much as feares, or doubts what ever men doth vow for, or against.

LADY ORPHANT
Pray send to her to lend it you, and then you may shew it me.

MRS ACQUAINTANCE
I will try if she will trust me with it.

[Exit.

LADY ORPHANT Sola.
O Heaven, grant that the praise my Father gave this Lord whilst in the world he lived, prove not as curses to me his Child, so grieve his soul with my unhappy life.

[Exit.

SCENE IV

[Enter the **LADY BASHFULL**, and **MRS REFORMER** her woman; she being in years.

MRS REFORMER

Madam, now you are become a Mrs. of a Family, you must learn to entertain visitants, and not be so bashfull as you were wont to be, insomuch as you had not confidence to look a stranger in the face, were they never so mean persons.

LADY BASHFULL

Alas Reformer, it is neither their birth, breeding, wealth, or title, that puts me out of Countenance; for a poor Cobler will put me as much out of Countenance as a Prince; or a poor Semestress, as much as a great Lady.

MRS REFORMER

What is it then?

LADY BASHFULL

Why there are unacustomated faces, and unacquainted humours.

MRS REFORMER

By this reason, you may be as much out of countenance as an unacustomed Dogg, or Cat, that you never saw before; or any other beast.

LADY BASHFULL

O no, for mankind is worse natured than beasts, and beasts better natured than men; besides beasts lookes not with censuring eyes, not heares, or listens with inquisitive eares, nor speakes with detracting tongues, nor gives false judgment, or spitefull censures, or slandering reproaches, nor jeeres, nor laughs at innocent or harmless Errours, not makes every little mistake a crime.

[Enter the Lady Bashfull's **PAGE**.

PAGE

Madam, there is a Coachfull of gallants allighted at the gate.

LADY BASHFULL

For heavens sake, say I have no desire to be seen.

MRS REFORMER

No, say my Lady is full of grief and is not fit to receive visits.

[Enter the **LADYES** and **GENTLEMEN**.

[Where at the **LADY BASHFULL** stands trembling and shaking, and her eyes being cast to the ground, and her face as pale as death.

[They speak to **MRS REFORMER**.

Where is the Lady Bashfull, pray Gentlewoman tell her we are come to kiss her hands.

[**MRS REFORMER** offers not to go forth.

LADY WAGTAILE
Will you do us the favour old Gentlewoman, as to let the Lady know we are here.

MRS REFORMER
If I am not so old as to be insensible, this is she.

LADY WAGTAILE
Is this she, alas good Lady, she is not well, for surely she hath a fit of an Ague upon her, she doth so shake; you should give her a Carduus-possit and put her to bed.

LADY AMOROUS
Lady, are you sick.

[She Answers not.

LADY WAGTAILE
She is sick indeed, if she be speechless.

MRS REFORMER
Madam, pray pull up your spirits, and entertain this honourable Company.

LADY WAGTAILE
Why is the defect in her spirits.

MRS REFORMER
She is young and bashfull.—

[They all laugh, except **SIR ROGER EXCEPTION**, and **SIR SERIOUS DUMB**.

Ha! Ha! She is out of countenance.

SIR ROGER EXCEPTION
No she is angry, because we are strangers unknown unto her; and she takes it for a rudeness that we are come to visit her, therefore let us be gone.

LADY AMOROUS
Let me tell you, it is meer shamefacedness.

SIR ROGER EXCEPTION
I say no, for those that are angry will shake extreamly, and turn as pale as death.

SIR HUMPHREY BOLD
Lady, take courage, and look upon us with a confident brow.

[All the while **SIR SERIOUS DUMB** lookes on the **LADY BASHFULL** with fixt eyes.

[The **LADY BASHFULL** offers to speak to the Company, but cannot for stuttering; they all laugh again at her.

MRS REFORMER
Lord, Madam! will you make your self ridiculous.

LADY BASHFULL
I cannot help it, for my thoughts are consumed in the fiery flame of my blushes; and my words are smothered in the smoak of shame.

LADY WAGTAILE
O! she speakes, she speakes a little.

MRS REFORMER
Pray Madam leave her at this time, and if you honour her with your Company again, she may chance to entertain you with some confidence.

LADY WAGTAILE
Pray let me and Sir Humphry Bold come and visit her once a day, if it be but halfe an hour at a time, and we shall cure her I warrant thee.

MRS REFORMER
I wish she were cured of this imperfection.

SIR HUMPHREY BOLD
She must marry, she must marry, for there is no cure like a husband, for husbands beget confidence, and their wives are brought a bed with impudence.

LADY WAGTAILE
By your favour Sir Humphry Bold, marriage must give way or place to courtship, for there are some wives as simply bashfull as Virgins; but when did you ever see, or know, or hear of courtly lovers, or Amorous courtships, to be bashfull: Their eyes are as piercing as light, and twinckles as Starrs, and their countenance as confident as day; and the discourses is freer than wind.

[He imbraces her.

SIR HUMPHREY BOLD
And your imbraces are wondrous kind.

LADY WAGTAILE
In troth we women love you men but too well, that is the truth of it.

SIR ROGER EXCEPTION
Pray Madam let us go, and not stay to anger this young Lady as we do.

LADY WAGTAILE
Farewell friend, Sir Humphry Bold and I will visit your Lady to morrow.

[As they were all going away, the **LADY WAGTAILE** turnes back again.

LADY WAGTAILE
Pray what may I call your name.

MRS REFORMER
My name is Reformer.

LADY WAGTAILE
Good Mrs. Reformer, I am heartily glad to see you well.

MRS REFORMER
I thank your Ladyship.

[All goeth away but **SIR SERIOUS DUMB**, and he stayes a little time to look upon the **LADY BASHFULL**, and then goeth out.

[Exit.

[The **LADY BASHFULL** Sola, and after they were all gone she stretches up her self.

LADY BASHFULL
O in what a torment I have been in; hell is not like it.

[Exit.

SCENE V

[Enter the **LADY ORPHANT**, and **MRS ACQUAINTANCE**.

LADY ORPHANT
Have you got the Picture?

MRS ACQUAINTANCE
Yes, but I have seen handsomer men in my opinion than this Picture doth represent.

[The **LADY ORPHANT** takes the Picture and views it with a stedfast eye.

LADY ORPHANT
I perceive you have no judgment in the Originall, nor skill in the Copy; for this Picture is most naturally penselled, the Painter hath drawn it so lively. That one may perceive his noble Soul to appear through his lovely, and lively Countenance; do but observe it well, and you will see as much as I.

MRS ACQUAINTANCE
That is impossible, unless I had your heart, for though my skill of the Copy, or shadow, may be as much as yours, yet my affections to the Originall is less; which makes my eyes not partiall.

LADY ORPHANT
What will the owner take for that Picture?

MRS ACQUAINTANCE
She will not sell it at any rate:

LADY ORPHANT
I wish she would, for I would buy it at any price.

MRS ACQUAINTANCE
She prizes it as highly as you, loving him as much; or well (as you do.)

LADY ORPHANT
How know you that?

MRS ACQUAINTANCE
Because I know she hath given him proofs of her love, which I believe you never did.

LADY ORPHANT
You mistake lust for love, ambition, for merit, I love not for the bodyes sake, but for the soules pure spirit.

[Exit.

ACT II

SCENE I

[Enter **TWO MERCHANTS**.

1ST MERCHANT
I hear the Lord Singularity hath given the Turkes a great defeat, he is both a wise, prudent, and valiant man.

2ND MERCHANT
Methinkes our Nation should not suffer such a person as he, to hazard his life in the service of other Countryes.

1ST MERCHANT
O it is an honour to our Nation, to let the world know what gallant men it breeds, besides our Nation is in peace with all the world; and he being active, hates to live idly, and dully at home, although he have a great estate, and is well beloved in his Country.

2ND MERCHANT

What command doth the Venetians give him?

1ST MERCHANT
He is a Generall, for he commands a great Army.

2ND MERCHANT
Is he marryed?

1ST MERCHANT
No, and it is reported he never will marry, but he loves Mistrisses well, which all Souldiers doth for the most part.

2ND MERCHANT
Then Italy is the best Countrey in the world for a souldier, there being the greatest store and most variety of Curtezans, for many of the Italians are, as many are in other Nations, rather Carpet-Knights, then fighting souldiers, they have more skill in setting musicall notes, than pitching a battle; in kissing a Mistrisses hand with a good grace, than shooting of a Cannon bullet with a great courage; they can take better aime at a window, than of an enemy. And though they often receive woundes, yet they are from fair Venus, not from cruell Mars.

1ST MERCHANT
But Mars souldiers when they skirmish in loves duels, receives woundes as often from fair Venus, as other men; and Italy hath as many gallant valliant men, bred and born in her, as any other Nation; and there are as many Carpet-Knights in other Nations, as in Italy ; and if valiant, and gallant men be indued with vertue, they are not the less to be esteemed; and as for Curtizans, all Nations is stored as much as Italy, but they do not so openly prefess it, as those in Italy doth.

2ND MERCHANT
For my part, I cannot think they are so good Souldiers as they were in Cæsars time.

1ST MERCHANT
That may be, for there is no such souldiers as Cæsars souldiers were, no not in the world; that is, there are no men so patient, obedient, carefull, industrious, laborious, daring, adventurous, resolute, and active, in these Warrs, in this age, as the Romans were in Cæsars time; and of all the souldiers, Cæsars souldiers were the best, and of all commanders Cæsar himself, yet those warriers was not less courtly to the feminine sex, than these of this age; and if you did talk with an understanding Souldier, he would tell you that Amors gave an edge to courage, and that it is a mark of a gallant man, and a brave souldier to be an Amarato ; and as for the Curtizans of Italy, if there can be an honest act in a dishonest life, it is that the Curtizans in Italy professes what they are; so that men are not deceived by them, nor betrayed into marriage; wherein other Nations men are cozened with counterfeit modesty, and drawn into marriage by pretended chastity, and then dishonoured by foul adultery, or shamed by marrying a private Curtizan, not knowing she was so.

2ND MERCHANT
I perceive by thee, that Merchants loves a Mistris as well as a Souldier.

1ST MERCHANT

Surely by thy talk thou art ignorant of thy own profession, which is to trade, and traffick into all Nations, and with all sorts; but yet, Merchants may be Souldiers if they will, and Souldiers may be Merchants if they please; but the truth is all men in the world are Merchants.

2ND MERCHANT
No, beggers are not.

1ST MERCHANT
But they are, for they traffick with prayers and praises for almes.

2ND MERCHANT
The best Merchants I know are Priests, for they trade into Heaven; and traffick with Jove.

1ST MERCHANT
That makes them so poor, for heavens commoditie are not saleable on earth.

[Exit.

SCENE II

[Enter the **LADY ORPHANT, NURSE FONDLY, FOSTER TRUSTY**.

LADY ORPHANT
Dear Nurse and Foster Father, grant to my desires and assist my designs.

NURSE FONDLY
What to let you wander about the world like a Vagabond, besides it is against the modesty of your Sex.

LADY ORPHANT
Are holy Pilgrimes Vagabonds, or is it immodest for the bodies of devout soules to travell to the sacred Tombe to offer penetentiall tears.

NURSE FONDLY
Why, you are no Pilgrime, nor is your journey to a godly end.

LADY ORPHANT
My journey will be to an honest end, for though I am loves Pilgrime, yet I shall travell to an honest heart; there to offer my pure affections.

NURSE FONDLY
To a deboist man, there to offer your Virginity.

LADY ORPHANT
Mistake me not, for though I love beyond a common rate, even to an extream degree, yet I am chastly honest, and so shall ever be; my grave shall witness my constancy.

[The **LADY ORPHANT** weeping. Exit.

FOSTER TRUSTY
Beshrew your tongue wife for speaking so sharply to our young Lady, she was left to our trust, care, and tender usage, and not to be snapt and quarrelled with.

NURSE FONDLY
Yes, and you would betray your trust to her childish folly.

FOSTER TRUSTY
Not that I would not, neither would I venture or yield up her life to loves melancholly.

NURSE FONDLY
Come, Come husband, you humour her too much, and that will spoile her I am sure.

[Exit.

SCENE III

[Enter **SIR PEACEABLE STUDIOUS** with a Book in his hand; a Table being set out, whereon is Pen, Ink and Paper. After he hath walked a turn or two, with his eyes fixt upon the ground, he sits down to the Table, and begins to write.

[Enter the **LADY IGNORANCE** his Wife.

LADY IGNORANCE
Lord Husband! I can never have your company, for you are at all times writing, or reading, or turning your Globes, or peaking thorough your Prospective Glasse, or repeating Verses, or speaking Speeches to your self.

SIR PEACEABLE STUDIOUS
Why wife, you may have my company at any time, Nay, never to be from me if you please, for I am alwaies at home.

LADY IGNORANCE
'Tis true, your person is alwaies at home, and fixt to one place, your Closet as a dull dead statue to the side of a wall, but your mind and thoughts are alwaies abroad.

SIR PEACEABLE STUDIOUS
The truth is, my mind sometimes sends out my thoughts like Coye ducks, to bring more understanding in.

LADY IGNORANCE
You mistake Husband, for your thoughts are like vain, or rather like false Scouts that deceives your understanding, imprisons your senses, and betrayes your life to a dull solitariness.

SIR PEACEABLE STUDIOUS
'Tis better to live a quiet solitary life, than a troublesome and an uneasie life.

LADY IGNORANCE
What is a man born for, but to serve his Countrey, side with his friends, and to please the effeminate Sex.

SIR PEACEABLE STUDIOUS
You say right wife, and to serve his Countrey, is to finde out such inventions as is usefull either in Peace or War; and to form, order and settle Common-wealths by Denizing Laws, which none but studious brains e're did, or can do. Tis true, practice doth pollish beauty and adorn, but neither layes the Foundation, nor brings the Materials, nor builds the walls thereof; and to side with friends, is to defend Right and Truth with sound arguments and strong proofs, from the tyrannical usurpation of false opinions, vain phantasmes, malicious satires, and flattering oratorie, and to please the effeminate Sex, is to praise their beauty, wit, vertue and good graces in soft Numbers, and smooth Language, building up Piramides of poetical praises, Printing their fame thereon, by which they live to After-ages.

LADY IGNORANCE
Prithy Husband mistake us not, for women cares not for wide mouthed fame; and we take more delight to speak our selves whilst we live, than to be talked of when we are dead, and to take our present pleasures, than to abstain our selves for After-ages.

SIR PEACEABLE STUDIOUS
Well wife, what would you have me do?

LADY IGNORANCE
Why, I would have you so sociable, as to sit and discourse with our friends and acquaintance, and play the good fellow amongst them.

SIR PEACEABLE STUDIOUS
What need we to have any other friends than our selves; our studies, books and thoughts.

LADY IGNORANCE
Your studies, books and thoughts, are but dull acquaintance, melancholly companions, and weak friends.

SIR PEACEABLE STUDIOUS
You do not wife consider their worth; for books are conversable, yet silent acquaintance, and study, is a wise Counsellor; and kind friends, and poetical thoughts are witty Companions, wherein other Societies and Companies are great inconveniences, and oftimes produces evil effects, as Jealousie, Adulterie, Quarrels, Duels, and Death, besides slanders, backbitings and the like.

LADY IGNORANCE
Truly Husband, you are strangely mistaken, for those Societies as I would have you frequent, doth Sing, Dance, Rallie, make Balls Masks, Playes, Feasts, and the like, and also makes Frollicks or Rubices, or Playes, at Questions and Commands, Purposes or Ridles, and twenty such like Pastimes and fine sports they have.

SIR PEACEABLE STUDIOUS
But surely Wife you would not like this kind of life, nor I neither; especially if we were in one and the same Company; for perchance you may hear wanton Songs sung, and see amorous glances, or rude or immodest Actions, and when you dance, have a secret nip, and gentle gripe of the hand silently to declare their amorous affections; and when you are at Questions or Commands, you will be commanded to kiss the men, or they you, which I shall not like, neither should you; or if they are commanded to pull of your Garter, which no chast and modest woman will suffer, nor no gallant man, or honourable husband will indure to stand by to see, and if you refuse, you disturb the rest of the Company, and then the women falls out with you in their own defence, and the men takes it as an affront, and disgrace, by reason none refuses but you; This causes quarrels with Strangers, or quarrels betwixt our selves.

LADY IGNORANCE
'Tis true, if the Company were not Persons of Quality which were civilly bred; but there is no rude Actions, or immodest behaviours offered or seen amongst them; Besides, if you do not like those sports, you may play at Cardes or Dice to pass away the time.

SIR PEACEABLE STUDIOUS
But Wife, let me examine you, have or do you frequent these Societies that you speak so Knowingly, Learnedly and Affectionately of?

LADY IGNORANCE
No otherwise Husband, but as I have heard, which reports makes me desire to be acquainted with them.

SIR PEACEABLE STUDIOUS
Well, you shall, and I will bear you company, to be an Eye-witness how well you behave your self, and how you profit thereby.

LADY IGNORANCE
Pray Husband do, for it will divert you from your too serious studies, and deep thoughts, which feeds upon the health of your body, which will shorten your life; and I love you so well, as I would not have you dye, for this I perswade you to, is for your good.

SIR PEACEABLE STUDIOUS
We will try how good it is.

[Exit.

SCENE IV

[Enter **NURSE FONDLEY**, and **FOSTER TRUSTY** her Husband.

NURSE FONDLY
How shall I keep your Journey secret, but that every body will know of it.

FOSTER TRUSTY

We will give out that such a deep melancholly have seized on her, since her Fathers death, as she hath made a vow not to see any creature besides your self for two years; As for me, I have lived so solitary a life with my solitary Master, this Ladies Father, that I have few or no acquaintance; besides, I will pretend some business into some other parts of the Kingdom, and I having but a little Estate, few will inquire after me.

NURSE FONDLY

So in the mean time I must live solitary, all alone, without my Husband, or Nurse-childe, which Childe, Heaven knows, I love better, than if I had one living of my own.

FOSTER TRUSTY

I am as fond of her, as you are, and Heaven knows, would most willingly sacrifice my old life, could it do her any service.

NURSE FONDLY

But we indanger her life, by the consenting to this journey, for she that hath been bred with tenderness and delicateness, can never indure the coldes and heats, the dirt and dust that Travellers are subject to; Besides, to be disturbed and broaken of her sleep, and to have ill Lodging, or perhaps none at all, and then to travel a foot like a Pilgrim: Her tender feet will never indure the hard ground, nor her young legs never able to bear her body so long a journey.

FOSTER TRUSTY

Tis true, this journey may very much incommode her, yet if she doth not go to satisfie her mind, I cannot perceive any hopes of life, but do foresee her certain death; for her mind is so restless, and her thoughts works so much upon her body, as it begins to waste, for she is become lean and pale.

NURSE FONDLY

Well! Heaven bless you both, and prosper your journey, but pray let me hear often from you, for I shall be in great frights and fears.

FOSTER TRUSTY

If we should write, it may chance to discover us, if our Letters should be opened, wherefore you must have patience.

[Exit.

SCENE V

[Enter the **LADY BASHFULL**, and **MRS REFORMER** her Woman.

LADY BASHFULL

Reformer, I am little beholding to you.

MRS REFORMER

Why Madam.

LADY BASHFULL

Why, you might have told a lye for me once in your life, for if you had not spoke the truth by saying I was the Lady, they came to see; they would never have guest I had been she; for they expected me to have been a free bold Entertainer, as they were Visitors, which is, as I do perceive, to be rudely familiar at first sight.

MRS REFORMER

But to have told a lye, had been to commit a sin.

LADY BASHFULL

In my conscience the Gods would have forgiven you, nay, they would have blest you; For it is a most pious and charitable act in helping the distressed; Besides, you had not only helped a present distress, but released a whole life out of misery; for as long as I live my thoughts will torment me: O! They wound my very soul already, they will hinder my pious devotions; For when I pray, I shall think more of my bashfull behaviour, and the disgrace I have received thereby, than of Heaven; Besides, they will starve me, not suffering the meat to go down my throat, or else to choke me, causing it to go awry, or else they will cause a Feaver; for in my conscience I shall blush even in my sleep, if I can sleep; For certainly I shall dream of my disgrace, which will be as bad as a waking memory: O! that I had Opium, I would take it, that I might forget all things; For as long as I have memory, I shall remember my simple behaviour, and as for my Page, he shall go, I am resolved to turn him away.

MRS REFORMER

Why madam?

LADY BASHFULL

Because he let them come in.

MRS REFORMER

He could not help it, for they followed him at the heels, they never stayed for an answer from you, or to know whether you were within or no, and there were a great many of them.

LADY BASHFULL

I think there was a Legion of them.

MRS REFORMER

You speak as if they were a Legion of Angels.

LADY BASHFULL

Nay, they proved a Legion of Divels to me.

MRS REFORMER

There was one that seemed to be a fine Gentleman, but he spake not a word.

LADY BASHFULL

They may be all what you will make them, or describe them, for I could make no distinction whether they were men or women, or beasts, nor heard no articulated sound, only a humming noise.

MRS REFORMER

They spake loud enough to have pierced your ears, if strength of noise could have done it, but the Gentleman that did not speak, looked so earnestly at you, as if he would have looked you thorough.

LADY BASHFULL
O that his eyes had that piercing faculty, for then perchance he might have seen; I am not so simple as my behaviour made me appear.

[Exit.

[Enter **SIR PEACEABLE STUDIOUS**, and the **LADY IGNORANCE** his Wife.

SIR PEACEABLE STUDIOUS
I have lost 500. pounds since you went in with the Ladies.

LADY IGNORANCE
500. Pounds in so short a time.

SIR PEACEABLE STUDIOUS
'Tis well I lost no more: But yet, that 500. pounds would have bought you a new Coach, or Bed, or Silver Plate, or Cabinets, or Gowns, or fine Flanders-laces, and now its gone, and we have no pleasure nor credit for it, but it is no matter, I have health for it, therefore I will call to my Steward to bring me some more.

LADY IGNORANCE
No, do not so, for after the rate you have lost, you will lose all your Estate in short time.

SIR PEACEABLE STUDIOUS
Faith let it go, 'tis but begging or starving after it is gone, for I have no trade to live by, unless you have a way to get a living, have you any.

LADY IGNORANCE
No truly Husband, I am a shiftless creature.

SIR PEACEABLE STUDIOUS
Yes, but you may play the Whore, and I the Shark, so live by couzening and cheating.

LADY IGNORANCE
Heaven defend Husband.

SIR PEACEABLE STUDIOUS
Or perchance some will be so charitable to give us suck'd bones from stinking breaths, and rotten teeth, or greasie scraps from fowl hands; But go wife, prithy bid my Steward send me 500. pounds more, or let it alone, I will run on the score, and pay my losings at a lump.

LADY IGNORANCE

No dear Husband, play no more.

SIR PEACEABLE STUDIOUS

How! not play any more say you, shall I break good Company with sitting out; Besides, it is a question whether I have power to leave off, now I have once begun; for Play is Witch-craft, it inchants temperance, prudence, patience, reason and judgment, and it kicks away time, and bids him go as an old bald-pated fellow as he is, also it chains the life with fears, cares and griefs of losing to a pair of Cards and set of Dice.

LADY IGNORANCE

For Heaven sake pitty me! If you consider not your self.

SIR PEACEABLE STUDIOUS

Can you think a Husband considers his wife, when he forgets, or regards not himself, when all love is self-love, for a man would have his Wife to be loving and chaste for his honours sake, to be thrifty for his profit sake, to be patient for quiet sake, to be cleanly, witty and beautifull for his pleasure sake, and being thus, he loves her; For if she be false, unkind, prodigal, froward, sluttish, foolish, and ill-favoured, he hates her.

LADY IGNORANCE

But if a Husband loves his wife, he will be carefull to please her, prudent for her, subsistence, industrious for her convenience, valiant to protect her, and conversable to entertain her, and wise to direct and guide her.

SIR PEACEABLE STUDIOUS

To rule and govern her, you mean wife.

LADY IGNORANCE

Yes, but a Husbands follies will be but corrupt Tutors, and ill Examples for a wife to follow; wherefore dear Husband, play no more, but come amongst the effeminate Societie, you will finde more pleasure at less charges.

SIR PEACEABLE STUDIOUS

Well wife, You shall perswade me for this time.

LADY IGNORANCE

I thank you Husband.

[Exit.

SCENE VII

[Enter the **LADY ORPHANT**, and **FOSTER TRUSTY**, as two Pilgrims.

FOSTER TRUSTY

My childe, you were best sit and rest your self, you cannot chose but be very weary, for we have travelled a great journey to day.

LADY ORPHANT
Truly I am as fresh, and my spirits are as lively, as if I had not trod a step to day.

FOSTER TRUSTY
I perceive love can work miracles.

LADY ORPHANT
Are not you Father a weary?

FOSTER TRUSTY
It were a shame for me to be weary, when you are not; But my childe, we must change these Pilgrims weeds, when we are out of our own Countrey; as when we are in Italy, otherwise we cannot pretend to stay in the Venetian Armie, but must travel as Pilgrims do to Jerusalem : But it were best we put our selves into Beggers garments until we come into the Armie, for fear we should be strip'd by Thieves; for I have heard, Thieves will strip Travellers, if their cloths be not all ragges.

LADY ORPHANT
'Tis true, and Thieves as I have heard, will rob Pilgrims soonest, finding many good Pilladge, wherefore we will accoutre our selves like to ragged Beggers.

[Exit.

ACT III

SCENE I

[Enter the **LADY BASHFULL**, as in a melancholly humour, and **MRS REFORMER** her Woman.

MRS REFORMER
Lord Madam! I hope you are not seriously troubled for being out of Countenance.

LADY BASHFULL
Yes truely.

MRS REFORMER
What? as to make you melancholly!

LADY BASHFULL
Yes, very melancholly, when I think I have made my self a scorn, and hath indangered my reputation.

MRS REFORMER
Your reputation! Heaven bless you, but your life is so innocent, harmless, chaste, pure and sweet, and your actions so just and honest, as all the Divels in Hell cannot indanger your reputation.

LADY BASHFULL

But spitefull tongues, which are worse than Divels, may hurt my reputation.

MRS REFORMER

But spite cannot have any thing to say.

LADY BASHFULL

Spite will lye, rather than not speak, for envie is the mother to spite, and slander is the Mid-wife.

MRS REFORMER

Why, what can they say?

LADY BASHFULL

They will say I am guilty of some immodest act, or at least thoughts, or else of some heynous and horrid crime, otherwise I could not be ashamed, or out of countenance, if I were innocent.

MRS REFORMER

They cannot say ill, or think ill, but if they could, and did, what are you the worse, as long as you are innocent.

LADY BASHFULL

Yes truely, for I desire to live in a pure esteem, and an honourable respect in every breast, and to have a good report spoke on me, since I deserve no other.

MRS REFORMER

There is an old saying, that opinion travels without a Passe-port, and they that would have every ones good opinion, must live in every mans age: But I am very confident, there is none lives or dyes without censures, or detraction; even the Gods themselves, that made man, hath given man power and free will to speak, at least to think what they will; That makes so many Athiests in thought, and so many several factions by disputation, and since the Gods cannot, or will not be free from censures, why should you trouble your self with what others say, wherefore pray put off this indiscreet and troublesome humour, for if you would not regard censure, you would be more confident.

LADY BASHFULL

I will do what I can to mend.

SCENE II

[Enter the **LADY ORPHANT**, and **FOSTER TRUSTY**, like two poor Beggers.

FOSTER TRUSTY

Childe, you must beg of every one that comes by, otherwise we shall not seem right Beggers.

LADY ORPHANT

If our necessities were according to our outward appearance, we were but in a sad condition; for I shall never get any thing by begging, for I have neither learn'd the tone, nor the Beggers phrase to move pity or charity.

FOSTER TRUSTY
Few Beggers move pity, they get more by importunity, than by their oratorie, or the givers charity.

[Enter **TWO GENTLEMEN**.

[She goeth to them and beggs.

LADY ORPHANT
Noble Gentlemen, pity the shiftless youth, and infirm old age that hath no means to live, but what compassionate charity will bestow.

1ST GENTLEMAN
You are a young boy, and may get your living by learning to work.

LADY ORPHANT
But my Father being very old, is past working, and I am so young, as I have not arrived to a learning degree of age, and by that time I have learn'd to get my living, my Father may be starved for want of food.

2ND GENTLEMAN
Why, your Father may beg for himself whilst you learn to work.

LADY ORPHANT
My Father's feeble legs can never run after the flying speed of pityless hearts, nor can he stand so long to wait for conscience almes, nor knock so hard to make devotion hear.

1ST GENTLEMAN
I perceive you have learn'd to beg well, though not to work, and because you shall know my devotion is not deaf, there is something for your Father and you.

2ND GENTLEMAN
Nay, faith boy, thou shalt have some of the scraps of my charity to, there is for thee.

LADY ORPHANT
Heaven bless you; and grant to you, all your good desires.

[**GENTLEMEN** Exit.

[Enter a **LADY** and **SERVANTS**.

LADY ORPHANT
Honourable Lady, let the mouth of necessity suck the breast of your charity to feed the hungry Beggers.

LADY

Away you rogue, a young boy and beg! You should be strip'd, whip'd, and set to work.

LADY ORPHANT
Alas Madam, naked poverty is alwaies under the lash of miserie, which forceth us to work in the quarries of stony hearts, but we finde the mineral so hard, as we cannot get out enough to build up a livelyhood.

LADY
Imploy your selves upon some other work then.

[**LADY** Exit.

[Enter a mean **TRADES-MAN**.

LADY ORPHANT
Good Sir relieve a poor begger.

TRADES-MAN
Faith boy, I am so poor, as I want relief my self; yet of what I have, thou shalt share with me; there is a peny of my two pence, which is all I have, and Heaven do thee good with it.

[**TRADES-MAN** Exit.

LADY ORPHANT
I perceive poverty pities poverty, as feeling the like miserie, where riches is cruel, and hard-hearted, not knowing what want is.

FOSTER TRUSTY
I perceive wit can work upon every thing, and can form it self into what shape it please, and thy wit playes the Begger so well, as we needed not to have stored our selves from our own Stocks, but have lived upon the Stocks of others.

LADY ORPHANT
But if all Stocks were as insipid as the Ladies, we should have starved, if we had not brought sap from our own home; But Father, I am weighed down with the peny the poor Trades-man gave me.

FOSTER TRUSTY
Why, it is not so heavy.

LADY ORPHANT
It is so heavy, as it burthens my conscience, and I shall never be at ease, not be able to travel any farther, until I have restored the peny to the giver again.

FOSTER TRUSTY
How should we do that, for it is as hard and difficult to find out that man, as to finde out the first cause of effects.

LADY ORPHANT
Well, I will play the Philosopher, and search for him.

FOSTER TRUSTY
But if you should meet him, perchance you will not know he was he.

LADY ORPHANT
O yes, for his extraordinary charity made me take particular notice of him.

[Enter the **TRADES-MAN** as returning back.

LADY ORPHANT
Most charitable and—

TRADES-MAN
What boy, wouldst thou have the other peny,

LADY ORPHANT
Most noble Sir, I have received from a bountifull hand, a summe of money, and since you were so charitable to divide the half of your store to me, so I desire I may do the like to you.

TRADES-MAN
No boy, keep it for thy self, and thy old Father; I have a Trade, and shall get more.

LADY ORPHANT
Pray take it for luck-sake, otherwise I shall never thrive.

TRADES-MAN
Faith I finde boy, thou art not as most of the World are; the more riches they get, the more covetous they grow.

LADY ORPHANT
Sir, pray take this.

TRADES-MAN
What do you give me here, a piece of Gold?

LADY ORPHANT
Yes Sir.

TRADES-MAN
That were extortion, to take a pound for a peny.

LADY ORPHANT
No, it is not extortion, since I can better spare this pound now, than you could your peny, when you gave it me; wherefore it is but justice,

TRADES-MAN
Well, I will keep it for thee, and when you want it, come to me again, and you shall have it: I live in the next street, at the signe of the Holy-lamb.

LADY ORPHANT
Pray make use of it, for I may chance never to see you more.

[Exeunt.

[Enter **SIR PEACEABLE STUDIOUS**, and the **LADY IGNORANCE** his Wife.

SIR PEACEABLE STUDIOUS
Faith Wife, with sipping of your Gossiping-cups, I am half drunk.

LADY IGNORANCE
Lord Husband! There were some of the Ladies that drank twice as much as you did, and were not drunk, and to prove they were not drunk, was that they talked as much before they drunk, as after; For there was such a confusion of words, as they could not understand each other, and they did no more, when they had drunk a great quantity of Wine.

SIR PEACEABLE STUDIOUS
That was a signe they were drunk, that they talked less, but how chance that you drank so little.

LADY IGNORANCE
Truly, Wine is so nauseous to my taste, and so hatefull to my nostrils, as I was sick when the cup was brought to me.

SIR PEACEABLE STUDIOUS
I know not what it was to you, but to me it was pleasant, for your Ladies were so gamesome, merry and kind, as they have fired me with amorous love ever since.

[Enter the Lady Ignorance's **MAID**.

MAID
Madam, the Lady Wagtail, and other Ladies, have sent to know if your Ladyship were within, that they might come and wait upon you.

[**SIR PEACEABLE STUDIOUS** chiks the maid under the Chin, and kisses her.

SIR PEACEABLE STUDIOUS
Faith Nan, thou art a pretty wench.

LADY IGNORANCE
What Husband? Do you kiss my maid before my face.

SIR PEACEABLE STUDIOUS
Why not Wife, as well as one of your sociable Ladies in a frollick, as you kiss me, I kiss Nan.

LADY IGNORANCE

So, and when Nan kisses your Barber, he must kiss me.

SIR PEACEABLE STUDIOUS

Right, this is the kissing frollick, and then comes the stricking frollick, for you strike Nan, Nan gently strikes me, and I justly beat you, and end the frollicks with divorce.

[Enter the **LADY WAGTAILE**, and other **LADIES** of the Societie, with the **LADY AMOROUS**.

LADY WAGTAILE

What? a man and his Wife dully alone together! Fie for shame.

LADY AMOROUS

Lawfull love is the dullest and drouziest companion that is, for Wives are never thought fair, nor Husbands witty.

SIR PEACEABLE STUDIOUS

Your Ladyship is learned in loves Societies.

LADY AMOROUS

Yes that I am, for I have observed, that if there be a match'd company, every man having a woman, their conversation is dull, every mans tongue whispering in his Mistriss eare, whilst the women are mute, listening to that which is whispered unto them; but let there be but one man amongst a company of women, and then their tongues runs races, striving with each other, which shall catch that one man, as the only prize, when the weaker wits runs themselves straite out of breath.

SIR PEACEABLE STUDIOUS

And must that one man run against them all.

LADY AMOROUS

O yes? and many times his wit beats them all.

SIR PEACEABLE STUDIOUS

Faith Lady? They must not be such strong winded wits as yours is, which is able to beat a dozen Masculine wits out of the field.

LADY AMOROUS

You are pleased to give me a complement.

[The **LADY IGNORANCE** seems melancholly.

LADY WAGTAILE

The merry God have mercy on you? What makes you so melancholly.

LADY IGNORANCE

I am not well to day.

LADY WAGTAIL

If you are troubled with melancholly vapours, arising from crude humours, you must take as soon as you wake after your first sleep, a draught of Wormwood-wine, then lye to sleep again, and then half an hour before you rise, drink a draught of Jelley-broth, and after you have been up an hour and half, eate a White-wine-caudle, then a little before a dinner, take a Toste and Sack, and at your meals, two or three good glasses of Clarret-wine; as for your Meats, you must eate those of light digestion, as Pheasant, Partridges, Cocks, Snipes, Chickens, young Turkies, Pea-chickens and the like; And in the After-noon, about four or five a clock, you must take Naples-bisket dip'd in Ippocrass, which helps digestion much, and revives the spirits, and makes one full of discourse, and not only to discourse, but to discourse wittily, and makes one such good company, as invites acquaintance, and ties friendship.

[The whilst the **LADY WAGTAIL** talks to the Lady Ignorance, she eyes her **HUSBAND**, who seems to court the **LADY AMOROUS**.

LADY AMOROUS

Faith I will tell your Wife what you say.

LADY WAGTAIL

That is fowl play, and not done like one of the Society, especially when my Lady is not well.

LADY AMOROUS

What? Is she sick! I lay my life she hath eate too much Branne Sturgeon, or Sammon without muskadine or Sack, or Neats-tongues, Bakon and Anchoves, Caveare, or Lobsters, without Rhenish-wines, or Oysters, or Sausages without Clarret-wine, or hath she eaten Potatoe-pies without dates, Ringo-roots, Marrow and Chestnuts, have you not? i faith confess.

LADY IGNORANCE

No indeed.

LADY AMOROUS

Why? I hope you have not taken a surfeit of White-meats, those childish meats, or with Water-grewel, Ponado, Barley-grevvel, those Hodge-podgely meats.

LADY IGNORANCE

Neither.—

LADY AMOROUS

Why, then you have over-heated your self with dancing or fretting and vexing your self at your ill fortune at Cards; or your Tayler hath spoiled some Gown, or your Coach-man was out of the way when you would go abroad; is it not so.

LADY IGNORANCE

No.

LADY AMOROUS

Why? Then your Husband hath crost some design, or hath angered you some other way!

[The **LADY IGNORANCE** blushes.

[They **ALL** laugh, and speak at one time; She blushes, She blushes.

LADY WAGTAIL
Faith Amorous, thou hast found it out! Sir Peaceable Studious you are to be chidden to anger your Wife; wherefore tell us how you did anger her, when you did anger her, and for what you did anger her.

SIR PEACEABLE STUDIOUS
Dear, sweet, fine, fair Ladies! be not so cruel to me, as to lay my Wives indisposition to my charge.

LADY WAGTAILE
But we will, and we will draw up an Accusation against you, unless you confess, and ask pardon.

SIR PEACEABLE STUDIOUS
Will you accuse me without a Witness?

LADY WAGTAIL
Yes, and condemne you too.

SIR PEACEABLE STUDIOUS
That were unjust! if Ladies could be unjust.

LADY AMOROUS
O Madam! we have a witness? her blushing is a sufficient witness to accuse him; Besides, her melancholly silence will help to condemn him.

LADY IGNORANCE
Pardon me Ladies, for when any of our Sex are offended, or angered, whether they have cause or not, they will rail louder than Joves thunder.

LADY AMOROUS
So will you in time.

LADY WAGTAIL
Let us jumble her abroad; Come Madam! we will put you out of your dull humour.

LADY IGNORANCE
No Madam? Pray excuse me to day; in truth I am not well.

LADY AMOROUS
No, let us let my Lady alone, but let us take her Husband, and tutour him

SIR PEACEABLE STUDIOUS
Ladies, give me leave to praise my self, and let me tell you? I am as apt a Scholar, as ever you met with, and as willing to learn.

LADY AMOROUS

Farewell Madam, we will order Sir P. Studious, and try what disposition he is of, and how apt to be instructed.

LADY IGNORANCE
Pray do Madam, he promiseth well.

[Exit.

[Enter **FOSTER TRUSTY**, and the **LADY ORPHANT**.

LADY ORPHANT
Now we are come into the Armie, how shall we demean our selves like poor Beggers.

FOSTER TRUSTY
By no means, for though you beg well, yet you will never get what you come for with begging, for there is an old saying, that although all charity is love, yet all love is not charity.

LADY ORPHANT
It were the greatest charity in the World, for him to love me; for without his love, I shall be more miserable than poverty can make me.

FOSTER TRUSTY
But poverty is so scorned and hated, that no person is accepted which she presents; Nay, poverty is shunn'd more than the Plague.

LADY ORPHANT
Why? it is not infectious.

FOSTER TRUSTY
Yes faith, for the relieving of necessity, is the way to be impoverished.

LADY ORPHANT
But their rewards are the greater in Heaven.

FOSTER TRUSTY
'Tis true, but their Estates are less on earth.

LADY ORPHANT
But blessings are more to be desired than wealth.

FOSTER TRUSTY
Well? Heaven bless us, and send us such fortune, that our long journey may prove successfull, and not profitless, and because Heaven never gives blessings, unless we use a prudent industry; you shall put your self into good clothes, and I will mix my self with his followers and servants, and tell them, as I may

truely, that you are my Son, for no mans Son but mine you are, was so importunate, as you would never let me rest, until I brought you to see the Lord Singularity, and they will tell him, to let him know his fame is such, as even young children adore him, taking a Pilgrimage to see him, and he out of a vain-glory will desire to see you.

LADY ORPHANT
But what advantage shall I get by that.

[Enter the **LORD SINGUALRITY**, and many **COMMANDERS** attending him.

FOSTER TRUSTY
Peace! here is the General.

COMMANDER
The enemie is so beaten, as now they will give us some time to breath our selves.

GENERAL
They are more out of breath than we are, but the States are generous enemies, if they give them leave to fetch their wind, and gather strength again.

LADY ORPHANT
Father, stand you by, and let me speak.

[She goeth to the **GENERAL**, and speaks to him.

Heaven bless your Excellencie.

GENERAL
From whence comest thou boy?

LADY ORPHANT
From your native Countrey.

GENERAL
Cam'st thou lately?

LADY ORPHANT
I am newly arrived.

GENERAL
Pray how is my Countrey, and Countrey-men, live they still in happy peace, and flourishing with plenty.

LADY ORPHANT
There is no noise of war, or fear of famine.

GENERAL
Pray Jove continue it.

LADY ORPHANT
It is likely so to continue, unless their pride and luxurie begets a factious childe, that is born with war, and fed with ruine.

GENERAL
Do you know what faction is?

LADY ORPHANT
There is no man that lives, and feels it not, the very thoughts are factious in the mind, and in Rebellious passions arises warring against the soul.

GENERAL
Thou canst not speak thus by experience boy, thou art too young, not yet a mans Estate.

LADY ORPHANT
But children have thoughts, and said to have a rational soul, as much as those that are grown up to men; but if souls grow as bodies doth, and thoughts increases with their years, then may the wars within the mind be like to School-boys quarrels, that falls out for a toy, and for a toy are friends.

GENERAL
Thou speakest like a Tutour, what boyish thoughts so ever thou hast; but tell me boy? what mad'st thee travel so great a journey.

LADY ORPHANT
For to see you.

GENERAL
To see me boy!

LADY ORPHANT
Yes, to see you Sir; for the Trumpet of your praise did sound so loud, it struck my ears, broke open my heart, and let desire forth, which restless grew until I travelled hither.

GENERAL
I wish I had merits to equal thy weary steps, or means for to reward them.

LADY ORPHANT
Your presence hath sufficiently rewarded me.

GENERAL
Could I do thee any service boy?

LADY ORPHANT
A bounteous favour you might do me Sir?

GENERAL
What is that boy?

LADY ORPHANT
To let me serve you, Sir.

GENERAL
I should be ingratefull to refuse thee, chose thy place.

LADY ORPHANT
Your Page, Sir, if you please.

GENERAL
I accept of thee most willingly.

Captain.:
But Sir? may not this boy be a lying, couzening, flattering dissembling, treacherous boy.

GENERAL
Why Captain, there is no man that keeps many servants, but some are lyers, and some treacherous, and all flatterers; and a Master receives as much injurie from each particular, as if they were joyned in one.

LADY ORPHANT
I can bring none that will witness for my truth, or be bound for my honesty, but my own words.

GENERAL
I desire none, boy, for thy tongue sounds so sweetly, and thy face looks so honestly, as I cannot but take, and trust thee.

LADY ORPHANT
Heaven bless your Excellence, and fortune prosper you, for your bounty hath been above my hopes, and equal to my wishes.

GENERAL
What is thy name?

LADY ORPHANT
Affectionata my Noble Lord.

GENERAL
Then follow me Affectionata.

[Exit.

ACT IV

SCENE I

[Enter the **LADY BASHFULL**, and **MRS REFORMER** her woman.

[Enter **PAGE**.

PAGE
Madam, there was a Gentleman gave me this Letter, to deliver to your Ladyships hands.

LADY BASHFULL
A Letter! pray Reformer open it, and read it, for I will not receive Letters privately.

[**PAGE** Exit.

MRS REFORMER
The superscription is for the Right Honourable, the Lady Bashfull; these present.
[The Letter.
MADAM,
Since I have had the honour to see you, I have had the unhappiness to think my self miserable, by reason I am deprived of speech, that should plead my suit, but if an affectionate soul, chaste thoughts, lawfull desires, and a fervent heart can plead without speech, let me beg your favour to accept of me for your servant; and what I want in Language, my industrious observance, and diligent service shall supply; I am a Gentleman, my breeding hath been according to my birth, and my Estate is sufficient to maintain me according to both; As for your Estate, I consider it not, for were you so poor of fortunes goods, as you had nothing to maintain you, but what your merit might challenge out of every purse; yet if you were mine, I should esteem you richer than the whole World, and I should love you, as Saints love Heaven, and adore you equal to a Dietie; for I saw so much sweetness of nature, nobleness of soul, purity of thoughts, and innocency of life, thorough your Bashfull countenance, as my soul is wedded thereunto, and my mind so restless; therefore, that unless I may have hopes to injoy you for my Wife; I shall dye,
Your distracted Servant,
SERIOUS DUMB.

LADY BASHFULL
Now Reformer, what say you to this Letter?

MRS REFORMER
I say it is a good honest, hearty affectionate Letter, and upon my life, it is the Gentleman I commended so; he that looked so seriously on you; and your Ladyship may remember, I said he viewed you, as if he would have looked you thorough, and you made answer, that you wished he could, that he might see you were not so simple, as your behaviour made you appear, and now your wish is absolved.

LADY BASHFULL
What counsel will you give me in this cause?

MRS REFORMER
Why? write him a civil answer.

LADY BASHFULL
Why should I hold corespondence with any man, either by Letter, or any other way, since I do not intend to marry.

MRS REFORMER
Not marry?

LADY BASHFULL
No, not marry.

MRS REFORMER
Why so?

LADY BASHFULL
Because I am now Mistriss of my self, and fortunes, and have a free liberty; and who that is free, if they be wise, will make themselves slaves, subjecting themselves to anothers humour, unless they were fools, or mad, and knew not how to chose the best and happiest life.

MRS REFORMER
You will change this opinion, and marry, I dare swear.

LADY BASHFULL
Indeed I will not swear, but I think I shall not, for I love an easie, peaceable and solitary life, which none injoys but single persons; for in marriage, the life is disturbed with noise and company, troublesome imployments, vex'd with crosses, and restless with cares; Besides, I could not indure to have Parteners to share of him, whom my affections had set a price upon, or my merit, or beauty, or wealth, or vertue had bought.

MRS REFORMER
So, I perceive you would be jealouse, if you were married.

LADY BASHFULL
Perchance I might have reason, but to prevent all inconveniences, and discontents, I will live a single life.

MRS REFORMER
Do what likes you best, for I dare not perswade you any way, for fear my advice should not prove to the best.

[Exeunt.

SCENE II

[Enter **AFFECTIONATA**, and **FOSTER TRUSTY**.

FOSTER TRUSTY
Now you are placed according to your desire, what wil you command me to do?

AFFECTIONATA

Dear Foster Father, although I am loth to part from you, yet by reason I shall suffer in my estate, I must intreat you to return home, for my Nurse your wife, hath not skill to manage that fortune my Father left me; for she knows not how to let Leases, to set Lands, to receive Rents, to repair Ruines, to disburst Charges, and to order those affairs as they should be ordered; which your knowledge, industry and wisdom will dispose and order for my advantage.

FOSTER TRUSTY
But how if you be discovered.

AFFECTIONATA
Why, if I should, as I hope I shall not, yet the Lord Singularity is so noble a person, as he will neither use me uncivily, nor cruelly.

FOSTER TRUSTY
All that I fear is, if you should be discovered, he should use you too civilly.

AFFECTIONATA
That were to use me rudely, which I am confident he will not do, and I am confident that you do believe I will receive no more civillity (if you call it so) than what honour will allow and approve of.

FOSTER TRUSTY
But jealousie will creep into the most confident breasts sometimes, yet I dare trust you, though I fear him.

AFFECTIONATA
I hope there is no cause to fear him, or doubt me, wherefore dear Father, let us go and settle our affairs here, that you may return home to order those there.

SCENE III

[Enter **SIR PEACEABLE STUDIOUS**, and the Lady Ignorance his Wife, She being undrest, her mantle about her, as being not well.]

SIR PEACEABLE STUDIOUS
In truth wife, it is a great misfortune you should be sick this Term-time, when the Society is so much increast, as it is become a little Common-wealth.

LADY IGNORANCE
If there be so many, they may the better spare me.

SIR PEACEABLE STUDIOUS
'Tis true, they can spare your company, but how can you want their companies.

LADY IGNORANCE
You shall be my Intelligencer of their pastimes.

SIR PEACEABLE STUDIOUS
That I will wife, but it will be but a dull recreation, only to hear a bare relation.

LADY IGNORANCE
As long as you partake of their present pleasures, and pleasant actions, what need you take care for me.

SIR PEACEABLE STUDIOUS
Yes, but I must in Justice, for since you have cured me of a studious Lethargie, I ought to do my indeavour to divert your melancholly; and there is no such remedy as the Society; wherefore dear wife, fling off this melancholly sickness, or sick melancholly, and go amongst them; for surely your sickness is in your mind, not in your body.

[She cries.

SIR PEACEABLE STUDIOUS
What, do you cry Wife, who hath angered you?

LADY IGNORANCE
Why you.

SIR PEACEABLE STUDIOUS
Who, I anger'd you! why I would not anger a woman, no, not my Wife for the whole World, If I could possible avoid it, which I fear cannot be avoided; for if I should please one of your Sex, I should be sure to displease another:—But that is my comfort, it is not my fault; but dear Wife, how have I offended you.

LADY IGNORANCE
Why did you kiss my maid before my face.

SIR PEACEABLE STUDIOUS
Why did you perswade me.

LADY IGNORANCE
Did I perswade you to kiss my maid.

SIR PEACEABLE STUDIOUS
No, but you did perswade me to be one of the Society, and there is kissing, and I thought it was as well to kiss your maid before your face, as a sociable Lady before your face.

LADY IGNORANCE
And why do you make love to the Ladies, since I suffer none to make love to me.

SIR PEACEABLE STUDIOUS
No, for if you did, I would fling you to death, to be imbraced in his cold arms; Besides, those actions that are allowable and seemly, as manly in men, are condemned in women, as immodest, and unbecoming, and dishonourable; but talking to you, I shall miss of the pleasant sports, and therefore, if you will go, come, the Coach is ready.

LADY IGNORANCE
No, I will not go.

SIR PEACEABLE STUDIOUS
Then I will go without you.

LADY IGNORANCE
No, pray Husband go no more thither.

SIR PEACEABLE STUDIOUS
How! not to go? nor to go no more, would you disswade me from that which you perswaded me to; Nay, so much as I could never be quiet, disturbing my harmless studies, and happy mind, crossing my pleasing thoughts with complaining words, but I perceive you grow jealouse, and now you are acquainted, you have no more use of me, but would be glad to quit my company, that you may be more free abroad.

LADY IGNORANCE
No Husband, truely I will never go abroad, but will inancor my self in my own house, so you will stay at home, and be as you were before, for I see my own follies, and am ashamed of my self, that you should prove me such a fool.

SIR PEACEABLE STUDIOUS
Do you think me so wise and temperate a man, as I can on a sudden quit vain pleasures, and lawfull follies.

LADY IGNORANCE
Yes, or else you have studied to little purpose.

SIR PEACEABLE STUDIOUS
Well, for this day I will stay at home, and for the future-time I will consider.

[Exeunt.

SCENE IV

[Enter **TWO SERVANTS** of the Generals.

1ST SERVANT
This boy that came but the other day, hath got more of my Lords affection, than we that have served him this many years.

2ND SERVANT
New-comers are alwaies more favoured than old waiters; for Masters regards old Servants no more, than the Imagerie in an old suit of Hangings, which are grown threed-bare with time, and out of fashion with change; Besides, new Servants are more industrious and diligent than old; but when he hath been here a little while, he will be as lazie as the rest, and then he will be as we are.

1ST SERVANT

I perceive my Lord delights to hear him talk, for he will listen very a tentively to him, but when we offer to speak, he bids us to be silent.

2ND SERVANT

I wonder he should, for when we speak, it is with gravity, and our discourse is sententious, but his is meer squibs.

[Enter **AFFECTIONATA**.

AFFECTIONATA

Gentlemen, my Lord would have one of you to come to him.

1ST SERVANT

Why, I thought you could supply all our places, for when you are with him, he seems to have no use of us.

AFFECTIONATA

It shall not be for want of will, but ability, if I do not serve him in every honest office.

1ST SERVANT

So you will make some of us knaves.

AFFECTIONATA

I cannot make you knaves, unless you be willing to be knaves your selves.

2ND SERVANT

What, do you call me knave?

AFFECTIONATA

I do not call you so.

[Exit.

2ND SERVANT

Well, I will be revenged, if I live.

[Exit.

SCENE V

[Enter the **LADY BASHFULL**, and **MRS REFORMER** her woman.

MRS REFORMER

Madam, I have inquired what this Sir Serious Dumb is, and 'tis said he is one of the finest Gentlemen in this Kingdom, and that his valour hath been proved in the wars, and that he is one that is very active and dexterous in all manly exercises, as riding, fencing, vaulting, swimming, and the like, Also that he is full of inventions, and a rare Poet, and that he hath a great Estate, only that he is dumb, and hath been so this twelve years and upwards.

LADY BASHFULL
Mrs Reformer. What makes you so industrious to inquire after him, surely thou art in love withim.

MRS REFORMER
In my conscience I liked him very well, when he was to see you.

LADY BASHFULL
The truth is, he cannot weary you with words, nor anger you in his discourse, but pray do not inquire after him, nor speak of him; for people will think I have some designe of marriage.

MRS REFORMER
I shall obey you, Madam.

[Exeunt.

SCENE VI

[Enter the **LORD SINGULARITY**, and **AFFECTIONATA**.

[He strokes **AFFECTIONATA'S** head.

LORD SINGULARITY
Affectionata, Thou art one of the diligent'st boys that ever had.

AFFECTIONATA
How can I be otherwise, Sir, since you are the Governour of my soul, that commands the Fort of my passion, and the Castle of my imaginations, which are the heart, and the head.

LORD SINGULARITY
Do you love me so much?

AFFECTIONATA
So well my Lord, as you are the archetectour of my mind, the foundation of my thoughts, and the gates of my memorie, for your will is the form, your happiness the level, and your actions the treasurie.

LORD SINGULARITY
Thy wit delights me more, than thy flattery perswades; for I cannot believe a boy can love so much; Besides, you have not served me so long, as to beget love.

AFFECTIONATA

I have loved you from my infancy, for as I suck'd life from my Nurses breast, so did I Love from fames, drawing your praises forth, as I did milk, which nourished my affections.

LORD SINGULARITY
I shall strive; boy, to requite thy love.

AFFECTIONATA
To requite, is to return love for love.

LORD SINGULARITY
By Heaven? I love thee, as a Father loves a son.

AFFECTIONATA
Then I am blest,

[Exeunt.

SCENE VII

[Enter **TWO SOULDIERS**.

1ST SOULDIER
What is this boy that our General is so taken with.

2ND SOULDIER
A poor Begger-boy!

1ST SOULDIER
Can a poor Begger-boy merit his affections?

2ND SOULDIER
He is a pretty boy, and waites very diligently.

1ST SOULDIER
So doth other boys, as well as he, but I believe he is a young Pimp, and carries, and conveys Love-letters.

2ND SOULDIER
Like enough to, for boys are strangely crafty in those Imployments, and so industrious, as they will let no times nor opportunities slip them, but they will find waies to deliver their Letters and messages.

[Exeunt.

SCENE VIII

[Enter the Lady Bashfulls **PAGE**, and **SIR SERIOUS DUMB**, who gives a Note to the **PAGE** to read.

PAGE
Sir, I dare not direct you to my Lady, as you desire me in this Note, and if I should tell her, here is a Gentleman that desired to visit her, she would refuse your visit.

[**SIR SERIOUS DUMB** gives the young **PAGE** four or five pieces of Gold.

PAGE
I will direct you to the room wherein my Lady is, but I must not be seen, nor confess I shewed you the way.

[**PAGE**, and **SIR SERIOUS DUMB** Exeunt.

SCENE IX

[Enter the **LORD SINGULARITY**, and **AFFECTIONATA**.

LORD SINGULARITY
Come Affectionata, sit down and entertain me with thy sweet discourse, which makes all other company troublesome, and tedious to me, thine only doth delight me.

AFFECTIONATA
My Noble Lord? I wish the plat-form of my brain were a Garden of wit, and then perchance my tongue might present your Excellencies with a Posie of flowery Rhethorick, but my poor brain is barren, wanting maturity of time; yet what it doth afford, although but bracks or moss; if you command, I shall present them to you.

LORD SINGULARITY
Thou hast an eloquent tongue, (and a gentle soul.)

AFFECTIONATA
My Noble Lord, I have hardly learn'd my native words, much less the eloquence of Language, and as for the souls of all mankind, they are like Common-wealths, where the several vertues, and good graces are the Citizens therein, and the natural subjects thereof; but vices and follies, as the thievish Borderers, and Neighbour-enemies, which makes inrodes, factions, mutinies, intrudes and usurps Authority, and if the follies be more than the good graces, and the vices too strong for the vertues, the Monarchy of a good life falls to ruine, also it is indangered by Civil-wars amongst the passions.

LORD SINGULARITY
What passions indangers it most?

AFFECTIONATA
Anger, malice, and despair.

LORD SINGULARITY

Were you never angry?

AFFECTIONATA
I am of too melancholly a nature, to be very angry.

LORD SINGULARITY
Why? are melancholly persons never angry?

AFFECTIONATA
Very seldom, my Lord, for those that are naturally melancholly, doth rather grieve, than fret, they sooner wast into sighes, than fly about with fury; more tears flows thorough their eyes, than words pass thorough their lips.

LORD SINGULARITY
Why should you be melancholly?

AFFECTIONATA
Alas, nature hath made me so; Besides, I find there is not much reason to joy, for what we love, perchance it loves not us, and if it doth, we cannot keep it long, for pleasures passeth like a dream; when pains doth stay, as if eternal were.

LORD SINGULARITY
Thou art composed with such harmonie, as thy discourse is as delightfull musick, wherein the soul takes pleasure.

[Exeunt.

SCENE X

[Enter the **LADY BASHFULL**, **SIR SERIOUS DUMB** following her, where **MRS REFORMER** her Woman meets them.

MRS REFORMER
Madam, now the Gentleman is here, you must use him civilly, and not strive to run away from him, wherefore pray turn, and entertain him.

[The **LADY BASHFULL** turns to him, but is so out of countenance, and trembles so much, as she cannot speak, but stands still and mute; All the while he fixes his eyes upon her.

MRS REFORMER
Pray speak to him, Madam, and not stand trembling, as if you were like to fall.

LADY BASHFULL
My spirits is seized on by my bashfull and innocent fears, insomuch, as they have not strength to support my body without trembling.

MRS REFORMER
Sweet Madam, try to speak to him?

LADY BASHFULL
Honourable Sir? give me leave to tell you, that my bashfulness doth smother the senses and reason in my brain, and chokes the words in my throat I should utter, but pray do not think it proceeds from crimes, but an imperfection of nature, which I have strove against, but cannot as yet rectifie

[**SIR SERIOUS DUMB** Civily bows to her, and then gives **MRS REFORMER** his Table-book to read.

[She reads.
Madam,
He hath writ here, that had his tongue liberty to speak, all that he could say, would be so far below, and inferiour to what might be said in your praise, as he should not adventure to presume to speak.

LADY BASHFULL
I will presume to break my brain, but I will invent some ways to be rid of his company.

[He follows her, Exeunt.

ACT V

SCENE I

Enter the **GENERAL**, and sits in a melancholly posture. Enters **AFFECTIONATA**, and stands with a sad countenance. The General sees him.

LORD SINGULARITY
What makes thee look so sad, my boy?

AFFECTIONATA
To see you sit so melancholly.

LORD SINGULARITY
Clear up thy countenance, for its not a deadly melancholly, though it is a troublesome one.

AFFECTIONATA
May I be so bold to ask the cause of it.

LORD SINGULARITY
The cause is, a cruel Mistriss.

AFFECTIONATA
Have you a Mistriss, and can she be cruel?

LORD SINGULARITY

O! Women are Tyrants, they daw us on to love, and then denies our suits.

AFFECTIONATA
Will not you think me rude, If I should question you?

LORD SINGULARITY
No, for thy questions delights me more, than my Mistriss denials grieves me.

AFFECTIONATA
Then give me leave to ask you, whether your suit be just?

LORD SINGULARITY
Just, to a Lovers desires.

AFFECTIONATA
What is your desire?

LORD SINGULARITY
To lye with her.

AFFECTIONATA
After you have married her?

LORD SINGULARITY
Marry her saist thou, I had rather be banish'd from that Sex for ever, than marry one, and yet I love them well.

AFFECTIONATA
Why have you such an adversion to marriage, being lawfull and honest.

LORD SINGULARITY
Because I am affraid to be a Cuckold!

AFFECTIONATA
Do you think there is no chaste women?

LORD SINGULARITY
Faith boy, I believe very few, and those that are men, knows not where to find them out, for all that are not married, professes chastity, speaks soberly, and looks modestly, but when they are martyed, they are more wild than Bachalins, far worse than Satyres, making their Husbands horns far greater than a Stags, having more branches sprouts thereon.

AFFECTIONATA
And doth he never cast those horns?

LORD SINGULARITY
Yes, if he be a Widower, he casts his horns, only the marks remains, otherwise he bears them to his grave.

AFFECTIONATA
But put the case you did know a woman that was chaste; would not you marry her?

LORD SINGULARITY
That is a question not to be resolved, for no man can be resolved, whether a womam can be chaste or not.

[**AFFECTIONATA** fetches a greater sighe.

LORD SINGULARITY
Why do you sighe, my boy?

AFFECTIONATA
Because all women are false, or thought to be so, that wise men dares not trust them.

LORD SINGULARITY
But they are fools, that will not try, and make use of them, if they can have them; wherefore I will go, and try my Mistriss once again.

[Exeunt.

SCENE II

Enter the **LADY IGNORANCE**, and her **MAID**. She hears a noise.

LADY IGNORANCE
What a noise they make below, they will disturb my Husbands study; go and tell those of my Servants, that I will turn them away for their carelesness, as that they cannot place, set, or hold things sure, but let them fall to maké such a noise.

MAID
I shall.

[**MAID** Exit.

LADY IGNORANCE
It shall be my study how to order my house without noise, wherefore all my Servants shall be dumb, although not deaf, and I will take none, but such as have corns on their feet, that they may tread gently, and all my Houshold-vessel shall be of wood, for wood makes not such a noise when it chance to fall, or is hit against a wall, as metal doth, which rings like bells, when it is but touched, neither will I have Houshold-vessels of Earth, for earthen-pots, pans and the like; when they fall and break, sounds as if a stonewall fell.

[Exit.

SCENE III

Enter the **GENERAL** and **THREE** or **FOUR COMMANDERS**.

GENERAL
On my soul Gentlemen, the boy is an honest boy, and no wayes guilty of this you tax him for.

COMMANDERS
Pardon us, my Lord, for giving your Excellence notice that the States are jealouse of him for a Spie, but we do not any wayes accuse him.

GENERAL
Will the States examine him, say you?

COMMANDERS
So we hear, my Lord.

GENERAL
Well Gentlemen, pray leave me for this time, and I will take care the boy shall be forth-coming, whensoever the State shall require him.

COMMANDERS
Your Lordships humble Servants —

[**COMMANDERS** Exit. The **GENERAL** solus.

GENERAL
A Spie, it cannot be, for he is neither covetous, nor malicious, revengefull, nor irreligious, but I will try him.

[Exit.

SCENE IV

Enter the Lady Bashfulls **CHAMBER-MAID**, and **MRS REFORMER** her Gentlewoman.

CHAMBER-MAID
Mrs. Reformer, pray tell me who that handsome Gentleman is, which follows my Lady about?

MRS REFORMER
He is one that is Noble, and Rich, and is in love with my Lady.

CHAMBER-MAID

Truly it is the strangest way of wooing, that ever was, for my Lady goeth blushing out of one room into another, and he follows her at the heels: In my conscience my Lady is ashamed to sit down, or to bid him leave her company, and surely they must needs be both very weary of walking, but sure he will leave her, when it is time to go to bed.

MRS REFORMER
It is to be hoped he will.

[Enter the **LADY BASHFULL**, and **SIR SERIOUS DUMB** following her.

MRS REFORMER
Madam, you will tire your self and the Gentleman, with walking about your house, wherefore pray sit down.

LADY BASHFULL
What! To have him gaze upon my face.

MRS REFORMER
Why, your face is a handsome face, and the owner of it is honest, wherefore you need not be ashamed, but pray rest your self.

LADY BASHFULL
Pray perswade him to leave me, and then I will.

MRS REFORMER
Sir, my Lady intreats you to leave her to her self.

[**SIR SERIOUS DUMB** writes then, and gives **MRS REFORMER** his Table-book to read.

MRS REFORMER
He writes he cannot leave you, for if his body should depart, his soul will remain still with you.

LADY BASHFULL
That will not put me out of countenance, because I shall not be sensible of its presence, wherefore I am content he should leave his soul, so that he will take his body away.

[He writes, and gives **MRS REFORMER** the Book.

[**MRS REFORMER** reads. He writes, that if you will give him leave once a day to see you, that he will depart, and that he will not disturb your thoughts, he will only wait upon your person for the time he lives, he cannot keep himself long from you.

LADY BASHFULL
But I would be alone.

MRS REFORMER
But if he will follow you, you must indure that with patience, you cannot avoid.

[SIR SERIOUS DUMB goeth to the **LADY BASHFULL**, and kisseth her hand, and Exit.

MRS REFORMER
You see he is so civil, as he is unwilling to displease you.

LADY BASHFULL
Rather than I will be troubled thus; I will go to some other parts of the World.

MRS REFORMER
In my conscience, Madam, he will follow you, wheresoever you go.

LADY BASHFULL
But I will have him shut out of my house.

MRS REFORMER
Then he will lye at your gates, and so all the Town will take notice of it.

LADY BASHFULL
Why so, they will howsoever, by his often visits.

MRS REFORMER
But not so publick.

[Exeunt.

SCENE V

Enter the **GENERAL**, and **AFFECTIONATA**.

LORD SINGULARITY
Affectionata.
Thou must carry a Letter from me, to my Mistriss.

AFFECTIONATA
You will not marry her, you say.

LORD SINGULARITY
No.

AFFECTIONATA
Then pardon me, my Lord, for though I would assist your honest love by any service I can do, yet I shall never be so base an Instrument, as to produce a crime.

LORD SINGULARITY
Come, come, thou shalt carry it, and I will give thee 500. pounds for thy service.

AFFECTIONATA
Excuse me, my Lord.

LORD SINGULARITY
I will give thee a thousand pounds.

AFFECTIONATA
I shall not take it, my Lord.

LORD SINGULARITY
I will give thee five thousand, nay ten thousand pounds.

AFFECTIONATA
I am not covetous, my Lord.

LORD SINGULARITY
I will make thee Master of my whole Estate, for without the assistance, I cannot injoy my Mistriss, by reason she will trust none with our Loves, but thee.

AFFECTIONATA
Could you make me Master of the whole World, it could not tempt me to do an action base, for though I am poor, I am honest, and so honest, as I cannot be corrupted, or bribed there-from.

LORD SINGULARITY
You said you loved me?

AFFECTIONATA
Heaven knows I do above my life, and would do you any service that honour did allow of.

LORD SINGULARITY
You are more scrupulous than wise.

AFFECTIONATA
There is an old saying, my Lord, that to be wise, is to be honest.

[Exeunt.

SCENE VI

Enter **SIR PEACEABLE STUDIOUS**, and meets his Ladies **MAID**.

SIR PEACEABLE STUDIOUS
Where is your Lady?

MAID
In her Chamber, Sir.

SIR PEACEABLE STUDIOUS
Pray her to come to me?

MAID
Yes Sir.

[**SIR PEACEABLE STUDIOUS**, Exit. Enter another **MAID** to the first.

1ST MAID
Lord, Lord! What a creature my Master is become; since he fell into his musing again, he looks like a melancholy Ghost, that walks in the shades of Moon-shine, or if there be no Ghost, such as we fancie, just such a one seems her, when a week since, he was as fine a Gentleman as one should see amongst a thousand.

2ND MAID
That was because he kiss'd you, Nan.

1ST MAID
Faith it was but a dull clownish part, to meet a Maid that is not ill-favoured, and not make much of her, who perchance have watch'd to meet him, for which he might have clap'd her on the cheek, or have chuck'd her under the chin, or have kiss'd her, but to do or say nothing, but bid me call my Lady, was such a churlish part? Besides, it seemed neither manly, gallantly, nor civilly.

2ND MAID
But it shewed him temperate and wise, not minding such frivilous and troublesome creatures as women are.

1ST MAID
Prithy, it shews him to be a miserable, proud, dull fool.

2ND MAID
Peace, some body will hear you, and then you will be turn'd away.

1ST MAID
I care not, for it they will not turn me away, I will turn my self away, and seek another service, for I hate to live in the house with a Stoick.

SCENE VII

Enter the **GENERAL**, and **AFFECTIONATA**.

AFFECTIONATA
By your face, Sir, there seems a trouble in your mind, and I am restless until I know your griefs.

LORD SINGULARITY

It is a secret I dare not trust the aire with!

AFFECTIONATA
I shall be more secret than the aire, for the aire is apt to divulge by retorting Ecohes back, but I shall be as silent as the Grave.

LORD SINGULARITY
But you may be tortured to confess the truth.

AFFECTIONATA
But I will not confess the truth, if the confession may any wayes hurt, or disadvantage you; for though I will not belye truth by speaking falsely, yet I will conceal a truth, rather than betray a friend. Especially, my Lord and Master: But howsoever, since your trouble is of such concern, I shall not with to know it, for though I dare trust my self, yet perchance you dare not trust me, but if my honest fidelity can serve you any wayes, you may imploy it, and if it be to keep a secret, all the torment that nature hath made, or art invented, shall never draw it from me.

LORD SINGULARITY
Then let me tell thee, that to conceal it, would damn thy soul.

AFFECTIONATA
Heaven bless me! But sure, my Lord, you cannot be guilty of such sins, that those that doth but barely hear, or know them, shall be damned.

LORD SINGULARITY
But to conceal them, is to be an Actor.

AFFECTIONATA
For Heaven sake then keep them close from me, if either they be base or wicked, for though love prompt me to inquire, hoping to give you ease in bearing part of the burthen, yet Heaven knows, I thought my love so honourable placed on such a worthy person, and guiltless soul, as I might love and serve without a scandal, or a deadly sin.

LORD SINGULARITY
Come, you shall know it.

AFFECTIONATA
I'l rather stop my ears with death.

LORD SINGULARITY
Go, thou art a false boy.

AFFECTIONATA
How false a boy howsoever you think me, I have an honest soul and heart that is ready to serve you in any honest way, but since I am deceived, and couzened into love by false reports, finding the best of man-kind basely wicked, and all the World so bad, that praise nothing good, and strives to poyson vertue, I will inancor my self, and live on Antidotes of prayers, for fear of the infection.

LORD SINGULARITY
And I will not you pray for me?

AFFECTIONATA
I cannot chose, my Lord, for gratitude inforces me; First, because I have loved you, next, because I have served you; and give me leave to kiss your hand, and then there drop some tears at my departure.

[Weeping kneels down, and kisses her hand.

LORD SINGULARITY
Rise, you must not go away until you have cleared your self from being a spie.

AFFECTIONATA
I fear no accusations,

[Exeunt.

EPILOGUE

Noble Spectators, you have spent this day;
Not only for to see, but judge our Play:
Our Authoress sayes, she thinks her Play is good,
If that her Play be rightly understood;
If not, 'tis none of her fault, for she writ
The Acts, the Scenes, the Language and the Wit;
Wherefore she sayes, that she is not your Debtor,
But you are hers, until you write a better;
Of even terms to be she understands
Impossible, except you clap your hands.

Margaret Cavendish – A Concise Bibliography

Philosophical Fancies (1653)
Poems and Fancies (1653)
Philosophical and Physical Opinions (1655)
Nature's Pictures drawn by Fancie's Pencil to the Life (1656)
The World's Olio (1655)
Playes, (1662) folio, containing twenty-one plays including
Loves Adventures
The Several Wits
Youths Glory, and Deaths Banquet
The Lady Contemplation
Wits Cabal
The Unnatural Tragedy

The Public Wooing
The Matrimonial Trouble
Nature's Three Daughters, Beauty, Love and Wit
The Religious
The Comical Hash
Bell in Campo
A Comedy of the Apocryphal Ladies
The Female Academy
Plays never before printed (1668), containing five plays.
The Sociable Companions, or the Female Wits
The Presence
The Bridals
The Convent of Pleasure
A Piece of a Play
Orations of Divers Sorts (1662)
Philosophical Letters, or Modest Reflections upon some Opinions in Natural Philosophy maintained by several learned authors of the age (1664)
CCXI Sociable Letters (1664)
Observations upon Experimental Philosophy & Description of a New World (1666)
The Blazing World (1666)
The Life of William Cavendish, Duke, Marquis, and Earl of Newcastle, Earl of Ogle, Viscount Mansfield, and Baron of Bolsover, of Ogle, Bothal, and Hepple, &c. (1667)
Grounds of Natural Philosophy (1668)